Instant Vortex Air Fryer Oven Cookbook For Beginners

A Practical And Effective Guide To Healthy, Quick And Easy Instant Vortex Air Fryer Oven Recipes that Beginners Users Can Grill, Bake, Fry & Roast

Dana Sanders

Table of Content

Introduction

Air frying utilizes superheated cooling air instead of hot oil to create the same crunchy flavor and feel deep-fried food. It always traps juices within the crispy covering, except without the extra grease: it's faster, lighter, better, and a lot less effort.

Air fry, bake, roast, and reheat in a flash with the pre-programmed Smart Programs. Juicy chicken wings, crispy fries, onion rings, and more are all air fried. Cauliflower bites, garlicky peas, shrimp skewers, and chicken nuggets are roasted in the fryer, Calzones or mini pizzas baked in the fryer, soft cinnamon rolls baked in the oven, and chewy brownie bits baked in the oven. Alternatively, for lunch, reheat last night's meal.

Air Frying Basics

What is an air-fryer, and how does it work?

Air-fryers are tiny countertop convection ovens in their most common form. They easily heat a tiny internal basket to high temperatures. They even have a fan that circulates hot air around the cooking basket at a fast level.

What are the benefits of using an air-fryer for cooking?

1. Air frying is a safer method of cooking.

Food fried in an air-fryer is so much healthier than food cooked in a deep fat fryer. You can cook your food with little or no oil.

2. Air frying is a quick way of cooking.

The air-fryer's convection fan rapidly circulates superheated air around the cooking. Cooking will be 20-30% easier than utilizing a standard oven as a result of this.

3. Air frying will help you save money and electricity.

When you turn on the daily oven, you're heating a massive cavernous cooking space.

Air-fryers heat up faster, need less space to retain heat, and cool off faster because of the limited internal cooking space. As a consequence, the amount of electricity used is normally reduced.

An air-fryer may be a convenient and practical way to cook, heat, and reheat for those who do not have a full kitchen option.

It isn't to suggest that air-fried foods aren't delicious or crisp.

Features And Functions

How do air-fryers work?

The air-fryer isn't the same as a traditional fryer. That's the same as cooking in the oven. It does not prepare food as effectively as slow cooking or pan-frying.

Many versions do not need preheating, saving time and allowing food to be prepared quickly. They won't heat the kitchen as much as the oven would in hotter climates and temperatures.

What should be looked for in an air-fryer?

Unlike pressure cookers, air-fryers' sales will not be dominated by a single brand, such as Instant Pot. There are a few parameters and factors to keep in mind if you're looking for the best air-fryer for you.

Packing: Some versions have front drawers for loading and unloading the food, while others have a flip-top lid. Experts prefer drawer-style models for ease of use and security.

The user-friendliness: Is it easy to learn and use the controls? Perhaps you want the whole family to use an air-fryer. It should also be easy to remove and clean the basket.

Controls are essential. Most versions can be adjusted to temperatures up to 400 degrees Fahrenheit F, but some only have one. For leftovers, often people use a reheat button, as well as presets for chicken and fish.

Functionality: Is it possible to interrupt the cooking process to transform or stir the food? For certain iterations, the time and temperature must be reset.

Dimensions: Many countertop models are big enough for one or two people. If you're cooking with a large group, you'll need to make several batches or buy a larger model, which takes up a lot of space. Some models combine an air-fryer and a toaster oven, enabling you to conserve room by replacing the toaster oven.

Tips for Cooking in an Air-Fryer

- Stop overcrowding the basket to ensure even cooking. Overcrowding the basket increases the amount of time it takes to cook.

- Since the appliance has already been heated, the second batch can cook a little faster when cooking in batches!

- To stop burning and search for doneness, shake the vegetables at least halfway through cooking.

- To protect the outside of the fish from drying out, cook it at a lower temperature than recommended.

- Put skin side up for crispy skin. The top of an air-fryer heats up.

Best Use of An Instant Vortex Air-Fryer

It's easy to use, and it's also quick to vacuum. It comes with a maintenance guide and a security guidance manual. The cooking tray blends into the bottom of the air-fryer basket.

It was lightweight and easy to drive around. It's recommended that you leave at least 5" of space around the Instant Air-fryer.

The Vortex has Smart Programs, which have preset temperatures and cooking times.

Chips, chicken nuggets, cauliflower wings, and more can be air fried.

Bake light and fluffy cookies and pastries, scalloped potatoes, and more.

Roasted meat, pork, vegetables, fish, and more.

To serve leftovers, heat it without drying it out or overcooking it.

Broil for top-down cooking, melt cheese around nachos and serve with a French onion soup.

It should be dehydrated.

You may adjust the time or temperature of air frying without stopping the process. To set the time or temperature for cooking, press the Time or Temp button and rotate the dial until it clicks.

Meal Plan

This Air-fryer meal plan is designed to make your life EASY.

Once you try meal planning, you will never want to go back. Need more convincing? Here are just a few ways you will benefit from following this meal plan:

- Shopping for groceries is more effective. There will be no more last-minute runs to the supermarket for the evening's dinner.

- It helps you save time. You will avoid all the regular choices on what to make by planning ahead of time.

- Reduces waste by avoiding the need to purchase more ingredients at the store.

- Since they will help select the weekly meal plan order, the whole family is interested. They can also chip in and assist in the kitchen so that they know what's for dinner.

- It's interesting to learn new stuff. You will arrange some creativity and have fun preparing more "fresh to you" recipes if you plan your meals ahead of time.

Measurement Conversion and Time Charts

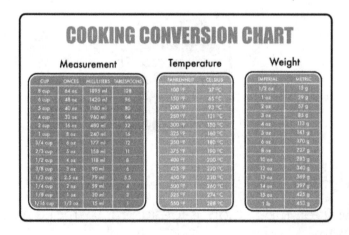

COOKING CONVERSION CHART

Measurement				Temperature		Weight	
CUP	ONCES	MILLILITERS	TABLESPOONS	FAHRENHEIT	CELSIUS	IMPERIAL	METRIC
8 cup	64 oz	1895 ml	128	100 °F	37 °C	1/2 oz	15 g
6 cup	48 oz	1420 ml	96	150 °F	65 °C	1 oz	29 g
5 cup	40 oz	1180 ml	80	200 °F	93 °C	2 oz	57 g
4 cup	32 oz	960 ml	64	250 °F	121 °C	3 oz	85 g
2 cup	16 oz	480 ml	32	300 °F	150 °C	4 oz	113 g
1 cup	8 oz	240 ml	16	325 °F	160 °C	5 oz	141 g
3/4 cup	6 oz	177 ml	12	350 °F	180 °C	6 oz	170 g
2/3 cup	5 oz	158 ml	11	375 °F	190 °C	8 oz	227 g
1/2 cup	4 oz	118 ml	8	400 °F	200 °C	10 oz	283 g
3/8 cup	3 oz	90 ml	6	425 °F	220 °C	12 oz	340 g
1/3 cup	2.5 oz	79 ml	5.5	450 °F	230 °C	13 oz	369 g
1/4 cup	2 oz	59 ml	4	500 °F	260 °C	14 oz	397 g
1/8 cup	1 oz	30 ml	2	525 °F	274 °C	15 oz	425 g
1/16 cup	1/2 oz	15 ml	1	550 °F	288 °C	1 lb	453 g

	Temperature (°F)	Time (min)		Temperature (°F)	Time (min)
Vegetables					
Asparagus (sliced 1-inch)	400°F	5	Onions (pearl)	400°F	10
Beets (whole)	400°F	40	Parsnips (½-inch chunks)	380°F	15
Broccoli (florets)	400°F	6	Peppers (1-inch chunks)	400°F	15
Brussels Sprouts (halved)	380°F	15	Potatoes (small baby, 1.5 lbs)	400°F	15
Carrots (sliced ½-inch)	380°F	15	Potatoes (1-inch chunks)	400°F	12
Cauliflower (florets)	400°F	12	Potatoes (baked whole)	400°F	40
Corn on the cob	390°F	6	Squash (½-inch chunks)	400°F	12
Eggplant (1½-inch cubes)	400°F	15	Sweet Potato (baked)	380°F	30 to 35
Fennel (quartered)	370°F	15	Tomatoes (cherry)	400°F	4
Green Beans	400°F	5	Tomatoes (halves)	350°F	10
Kale leaves	250°F	12	Zucchini (½-inch sticks)	400°F	12
Mushrooms (sliced ¼-inch)	400°F	5			
Chicken					
Breasts, bone in (1.25 lbs.)	370°F	25	Legs, bone in (1.75 lbs.)	380°F	30
Breasts, boneless (4 oz.)	380°F	12	Wings (2 lbs.)	400°F	12
Drumsticks (2.5 lbs.)	370°F	20	Game Hen (halved - 2 lbs.)	390°F	20
Thighs, bone in (2 lbs.)	380°F	22	Whole Chicken (6.5 lbs.)	360°F	75
Thighs, boneless (1.5 lbs.)	380°F	18 to 20	Tenders	360°F	8 to 10
Beef					
Burger (4 oz.)	370°F	16 to 20	Meatballs (3-inch)	380°F	10
Filet Mignon (8 oz.)	400°F	18	Ribeye, bone in (1-inch, 8 oz.)	400°F	10 to 15
Flank Steak (1.5 lbs.)	400°F	12	Sirloin steaks (1-inch, 12 oz.)	400°F	9 to 14
London Broil (2 lbs.)	400°F	20 to 28	Beef Eye Round Roast (4 lbs.)	390°F	45 to 55
Meatballs (1-inch)	380°F	7			

	Temperature (°F)	Time (min)		Temperature (°F)	Time (min)
Pork and Lamb					
Loin (2 lbs.)	360°F	55	Bacon (thick cut)	400°F	6 to 10
Pork Chops, bone in (1-inch, 6.5 oz.)	400°F	12	Sausages	380°F	15
Tenderloin (1 lb.)	370°F	15	Lamb Loin Chops (1-inch thick)	400°F	8 to 12
Bacon (regular)	400°F	5 to 7	Rack of lamb (1.5 - 2 lbs.)	380°F	22
Fish and Seafood					
Calamari (8 oz.)	400°F	4	Tuna steak	400°F	7 to 10
Fish Fillet (1-inch, 8 oz.)	400°F	10	Scallops	400°F	5 to 7
Salmon, fillet (6 oz.)	380°F	12	Shrimp	400°F	5
Swordfish steak	400°F	10			
Frozen Foods					
Onion Rings (12 oz.)	400°F	8	Fish Sticks (10 oz.)	400°F	10
Thin French Fries (20 oz.)	400°F	14	Fish Fillets (½-inch, 10 oz.)	400°F	14
Thick French Fries (17 oz.)	400°F	18	Chicken Nuggets (12 oz.)	400°F	10
Mozzarella Sticks (11 oz.)	400°F	8	Breaded Shrimp	400°F	9
Pot Stickers (10 oz.)	400°F	8			

Chapter No 1: Air-Fryer Breakfast

Recipes

1. Breakfast Sausage

Cook Time: 20 mins Servings: 8 Difficulty: Medium

Ingredients

- 1 tbsp. of maple syrup

- 1 lb of ground pork

- 1 tsp of sea salt

- 1 lb. of ground turkey

- 2 tsp of fennel seeds

- 2 tsp of garlic powder

- 1 tsp of paprika

- 2 tsp of dry-rubbed sage

- 1 tsp of dried thyme

Instructions

1. In a bowl, mix turkey and pork.

2. In another bowl, mix the rest of the ingredients.

3. Mix the spices with ground meat. Mix well.

4. Make 2 to 3 tbsp into balls and then make into patties.

5. Place into the basket of air-fryer in one even layer, and cook for ten mins at 370 degrees F.

6. Take out from the air-fryer and serve with English biscuits.

2. Air-Fried Radishes

Cook Time: 20 mins Servings: 6 Difficulty: Easy

Ingredients

- Radishes, trimmed & quartered 2-1/4 lbs. (about 6 cups)

- Olive oil 3 tbsps.

- Minced fresh oregano 1 tbsp/ dried oregano 1 tsp

- Salt 1/4 tsp

- Pepper 1/8 tsp

Instructions

1. Preheat the fryer to 375 degrees F. Toss the remaining products with the radishes.

2. In an air-fryer basket, put the radishes on an oiled tray. Cook till crisp-tender, 12-15 mins, occasionally stirring.

3. Air-Fryer Ham and Egg Pockets

Cook Time: 25 mins Servings: 2 Difficulty: Easy

Ingredients

- Large egg 1

- 2% milk 2 tsp

- Butter 2 tsp

- Thinly sliced deli ham 1 ounce, chopped.

- Shredded cheddar cheese 2 tbsps.

- refrigerated crescent rolls 1 tube (4 ounces)

Instructions

1. Preheat the fryer to 300 degrees F. Combine the egg & milk in a shallow bowl. Heat the butter in a small skillet till hot. Apply the egg mixture; cook & stir until the eggs are set, over med heat. From the heat, remove it. Fold in the cheese and ham.

2. The crescent dough is divided into 2 rectangles. Perforations of the seal; half spoon of filling down the middle of each rectangle.

3. Fold the dough over the filling, close with a squeeze. In the air-fryer basket, put it in one layer on an oiled tray. Cook until crispy brown, 8-10 mins.

4. Breakfast Stuffed Peppers

Cook Time: 20 mins Servings: 2 Difficulty: Easy

Ingredients

- olive oil: 1 tsp 1 bell pepper cut into half, remove seeds Sriracha flakes: 1 pinch   4 whole eggs

- Salt & pepper: 1 pinch of each

Instructions

1. Rub the cut side of bell pepper with oil.

2. Add 2 eggs in every half of pepper—season with your favorite seasoning.

3. Oil spray the Air-Fryer's basket.

4. Place peppers in the basket of the air-fryer without crowding the basket.

5. Cook for 15 mins at 330 degrees F, or till the eggs reached the desired consistency.

5. Air-Fryer Eggplant Fries

Cook Time: 10 mins/batch Servings: 6 Difficulty: Easy

Ingredients

- Large eggs 2

- Grated parmesan cheese 1/2 cup

- Toasted wheat germ 1/2 cup

- Italian seasoning 1 tsp

- Garlic salt 3/4 tsp

- Eggplant 1 medium (about 1 to 1/4 lbs.)

- Meatless pasta sauce 1 cup, warmed.

- Cooking spray

Instructions

1. Preheat the fryer to 375 degrees F. Whisk the eggs together in a bowl. Mix the cheese, wheat germ & seasonings in another bowl.

2. Trim the eggplant ends; cut the eggplant into 1/2"-thick slices lengthwise. Cut lengthwise to 1/2" slice strips. Dip the eggplant in the eggs, then fill with the mixture of cheese.

3. Arrange the eggplant in batches on an oiled tray in the air-fryer basket in a layer, dust with cooking spray. Now Cook until the brown is crispy, 4-5 mins. Turn; spritz with Spray for cooking. Cook until brown 4-5 mins. Serve with pasta sauce immediately.

6. Bacon & Egg Breakfast Bombs

Cook Time: 50 mins Servings: 8 Difficulty: Medium

Ingredients

- ¼ tsp of black pepper

- 4 bacon slices, slice into half" pieces

- 1 tbsp of butter

- 1 egg mixed with 1 tbsp of water

- 1/4 cup of sharp cheddar cheese

- 2 eggs, whisked

- Buttermilk biscuits, refrigerated (1 can) (5 biscuits)

Instructions

1. Cut out a parchment paper of Air-Fryer's basket size and place it in the basket and spray the paper with cooking spray.

2. In a skillet, cook bacon until it becomes crispy. Take out on a paper towel. Drain the fat.

3. Add butter into the skillet, melt the butter.

4. Whisk 2 eggs with black pepper.

5. Pour eggs into the skillet and cook until still moist. Turn off the heat and add bacon. Let it cool for five mins.

6. Separate 5 biscuits into two layers.

7. Add one tbsp of eggs into each biscuit. Add cheese on top.

8. Fold pinch the edges.

9. Brush each biscuit bomb with egg wash.

10. Place bombs in the basket of air-fryer seam side down in one layer.

11. Cook for 8 mins at 325 degrees F; cook for 4 to 6 mins more if required.

Chapter No: 2 Lunch

7. Weight Watchers Air-Fryer Mozzarella Cheese Sticks

Cook Time: 10 min Servings: 2 Difficulty: Easy

Ingredients

- Sargento Light String Cheese 1 package

- Italian breadcrumbs 1 cup

- Egg 1

- Flour 1/2 cup

- Marinara sauce 1 cup (for dipping, optional)

- Salt & pepper

Instructions

1. Add salt & pepper to the breadcrumbs in a bowl.

2. Add flour to 1 bowl, to another bowl, bread crumbs, and eggs to another bowl.

3. Dip the sticks of cheese into the flour, then the egg & breadcrumbs.

4. For around one hour, freeze cheese sticks - you want them to firm up.

5. Place the Air-Fryer at 400 degrees F. To the fryer, add the cheese sticks.

6. Cook, then flip, for 4 mins. Cook for an extra 4 mins.

8. Air-Fryer Sweet and Sour Pork

Cook Time: 15 mins Servings: 2 Difficulty: Easy

Ingredients

- Unsweetened crushed pineapple 1/2 cup, undrained

- Cider vinegar 1/2 cup

- Sugar 1/4 cup

- Packed dark brown sugar 1/4 cup

- Ketchup 1/4 cup

- Reduced-sodium soy sauce 1 tbsp

- Dijon mustard 1-1/2 tsp

- Garlic powder 1/2 tsp

- Pork tenderloin 1 (3/4 lb), halved.

- Salt 1/8 tsp

- Pepper 1/8 tsp

- Optional sliced green onions

- Cooking spray

Instructions

1. Combine the 1st 8 Ingredients in a saucepan. Get it to a boil; lower the heat. Simmer it uncovered, till thickened, 6 to 8 mins, occasionally stirring.

2. Preheat the fryer to 350 degrees F. Sprinkle salt & pepper on the pork. Place the pork in the air-fryer basket on a greased tray; spritz with the cooking spray. Cook for 7-8 mins before the pork starts to brown around the edges. Pour two tbsp of sauce over the pork. Cook until at least 145 ° F is read by a thermometer placed into the pork, 10 to 12 mins longer. Let the pork stand before slicing for 5 mins. Serve with the sauce that remains. Top with the sliced green onions if needed.

9. Puffed Egg Tarts

Cook Time: 20 mins Servings: 4 Difficulty: Easy

Ingredients

- All-purpose flour

- Frozen puff pastry 1 sheet

- Shredded cheese 3/4 cup such as Gruyère, Monterey Jack or Cheddar, divided

- Eggs 4 large

- Minced fresh parsley/chives 1 tbsp optional.

Instructions

1. To 390 degrees F, preheat the Air-Fryer.

2. Unfold the pastry sheet on a lightly floured surface. Break into 4 squares.

3. Put 2 squares in the basket of the Air-Fryer and space them apart. Air-fry for 10 mins or till medium golden-brown pastry.

4. Open the basket and press each square center down to create an indentation using a metal spoon. Sprinkle each indentation with 3 tbsp cheese and gently crack the egg in the middle of each pastry.

5. Air-fry for 7-11 mins or until the ideal doneness of the eggs. Move to a wire rack placed over waxed paper & allow 5 mins to cool. If necessary, sprinkle with half parsley. Serve it sweet.

6. With the left pastry squares, eggs, cheese, and parsley, repeat steps 2-4.

Chapter No: 3 Dinner Recipes

10.   Chipotle Steak Tacos

Cook Time: 8 mins Servings: 4 Difficulty: Easy

Ingredients

The Steak:

- Flank steak 1 ½ lbs

- Red Onion 1/2 cup

- Garlic 2 cloves crushed & peeled.

- Chipotle Chile in Adobo Sauce 1

- Ancho Chile Powder 1 tbsp

- Ground Cumin 1 tsp

- Dried Oregano 1 tsp

- Olive Oil 1 tbsp

- Kosher Salt 1 ½ tsp

- Ground Black Pepper 1/2 tsp

- Water 2 tbsp

For Serving:

- Salsa 1 cup

- Tortillas 8 flour, tortillas 6-inch, warmed.

- Cotija cheese 1/2 cup, crumbled.

Instructions

1. Put beef strips in the large bowl/resealable bag of plastic. In the blender/ food processor, mix chipotle chile, onion, oregano, chile powder, garlic, cumin,

olive oil, water, pepper, adobo sauce & salt. Blend till smooth. Put marinade on meat & mix/ seal bag & massage bag to thoroughly coat & mix. Marinate at room temp for thirty mins/cover & refrigerate for twenty-four hours.

2. Use tongs, remove beef strips from the bag & lay the basket of an Air-fryer. Minimize overlap as possible; remove marinade. Adjust Air-fryer at 400 degrees F for eight mins and flip beef strips in the center through cooking time. Do this in the batches.

For the oven

1. Put a steak on the sheet pan in a single layer.

2. Adjust oven to the broil & cook steak for three to four mins.

3. Turn & allow cook for an extra two mins.

11. Cilantro Pesto Chicken Legs

Cook Time: 20 mins Servings: 2 Difficulty: Easy

Ingredients

- Chicken drumsticks 4

- Cilantro 1/2 cup

- Jalapeño Peppers 1/2

- Garlic 8 cloves

- Ginger 2 thin slices

- Oil 2 tbsps.

- Lemon Juice 2 tbsp

- Kosher Salt 1 tsp

Instructions

1. Put drumsticks in the flat tray. Use the sharp knife's tip, cut small slashes in the chicken at steady intervals so the marinade can easily penetrate the chicken.

2. Equally chop pepper, ginger, cilantro, garlic & put them in a bowl.

3. Put oil, salt & lemon juice in the chopped vegetables & combine well.

4. Spread this combination on the chicken.

5. Allow chicken to marinate at least for thirty mins / up to twenty-four hours in the refrigerator.

6. When completely ready to cook, put chicken legs in the Air-fryer basket; skin must be side up.

7. Adjust Air-fryer at 390 degrees F for twenty mins for the meaty legs of chicken. In the center, turn the legs of the chicken over.

8. Use a meat thermometer to confirm that the chicken has touched the internal temp of 165 degrees F. Remove & serve with sufficient napkins.

12.   Crispy Pork Belly

Cook Time: 30 mins Servings: 4 Difficulty: Easy

Ingredients

- Pork belly 1 lb

- Water 3 cups

- Kosher Salt 1 tsp

- Ground Black Pepper 1 tsp

- Soy Sauce 2 tbsps.

- Bay Leaves 2

- Garlic 6 cloves

Instructions

1. Cut pork belly into three thick chunks so that it can cook evenly.

2. Put all of the ingredients in the inner liner of the Instant Pot/ pressure cooker. Cook pork belly at

maximum pressure for fifteen mins. Let the pot sit for ten mins & release the remaining pressure. Use a set of tongs, cautiously remove meat from the pressure cooker. Let meat drain & dry for ten mins.

3. Cut every three chunks of the pork belly into two long slices.

4. Put pork belly slices in the basket of Air-fryers. Adjust Air-fryer at 400 degrees F for fifteen mins/ till fat on pork belly has been crisped & then serve.

Chapter No 4: Air-Fryer Poultry, Brunch Recipes

13. Chicken drumsticks (air-fryer teriyaki)

Cook Time: 20 mins Servings: 6 Difficulty: Easy

Ingredients

- Chicken drumsticks 6 Teriyaki sauce 1 cup

Instructions

1. Combine drumsticks with the teriyaki sauce in the zip lock bag (gallon size). Let it marinate for thirty mins.

2. Air-fryer preheated to 360 degrees F. Put drumsticks in 1 layer in an air-fryer basket & cook for twenty mins. Shake your basket sometimes thru cooking.

3. Top with sesame seeds & mined green onions.

14.   Mediterranean Chicken Bowls

Cook time: 30 mins Servings: 4 Difficulty: Medium

Ingredients

- 1 lb of skinless chicken breasts, boneless, cut into one and a half" pieces

- 2 cups of cherry or grape tomatoes

- Dried oregano: 1 tsp

- Olive oil: 1 tbsp

- 1 cup of couscous

- Salt & pepper, to taste

- 1/4 cup of fresh dill

- Ground sumac: 1 tsp

- 1 chopped onion

- Grated lemon zest: 1 tsp + 1 tbsp of lemon juice

- For Servings: feta (crumbled)

Instructions

1. In a bowl, coat chicken with oil, half tsp salt and pepper, sumac, and oregano.

2. Add onions and tomatoes, mix well.

3. Place in the basket of air-fryer and cook at 400 degrees F, for 15-20 mins; shake the basket a few times until chicken is cooked completely and golden brown.

4. In the meantime, mix the couscous with zest and cook as per instructions on the package.

5. Fluff it and add in 2 tbsp of dill and lemon juice.

6. Serve couscous with vegetables and chicken. Top with feta and dill, enjoy.

15. Garlic parmesan chicken wings

Cook Time: 30 mins Servings: 3 Difficulty: Easy

Ingredients

- Chicken wings 1 1/2 lbs

- Sea salt 1/2 tsp

- Black pepper 1/2 tsp

- Smoked paprika 1/2 tsp

- Garlic powder 1/2 tsp

- Onion Powder 1/2 tsp

- Baking powder 1 tbsp

- Wings sauce garlic parmesan

- Melted & unsalted butter 1/4 cup

- grated parmesan 1/2 cup

- Onion powder 1 tsp

- Garlic powder 1 tsp

- Dried parsley 1 tsp

- Black pepper 1/4 tsp

Instructions

1. Take your chicken wing parts from a fridge & pat dry.

2. Mix the black pepper, paprika, sea salt, garlic powder, baking powder & onion powder in the dish/ramekin.

3. Drizzle the mixture of seasoning on the wings & toss to coat.

4. In the air-fryer, put wings on the flat layer.

5. Using an air-fryer programmed settings for the chicken, cook for 25 to 30 mins. Set your timer for around 15 mins, turn the wings, and then check your wings at 5 mins intervals till the skin becomes crispy.

To make the wings crispy very quickly requires turning them around halfway thru.

6. In the bowl, mix all the components for the sauce of the garlic parmesan.

7. Toss your wings in the mixture of garlic parmesan & serve immediately.

16.   Tender Chicken

Cook time: 18 mins Servings: 4 Difficulty: Easy

Ingredients

- 4 chicken bone-in thighs

- 1 ½ tbsp of canola oil

- 1 tbsp smoked paprika

- 1 ½ tsp of rosemary (dried)

- 1 ½ tbsp of mustard (whole-grain)

- Kosher salt & black pepper, to taste

- 1 lemon, juiced & zested

Instructions

1. Take a bowl and mix rosemary, mustard, lemon juice, paprika, and zest.

2. Coat the chicken in spices. Cover it and keep it in the fridge for 4 to 8 hours.

3. Let the air-fryer preheat to 400 degrees F.

4. Take chicken out from marinade.

5. Place the chicken in the air-fryer, in one even layer. Cook for 18 mins, and flip halfway through until internal chicken temperature reaches 160 to 165 F.

6. Rest the thighs in aluminum for five mins, then serve and enjoy.

17.   Crispy air-fryer chicken wings

Cook Time: 35 mins Servings: 4 Difficulty: Easy

Ingredients

- Chicken wings 2 lb Baking powder gluten-free 2 tsp

- Sea salt 3/4 tsp Black pepper 1/4 tsp

Instructions

1. In the bowl, toss your wings with sea salt, black pepper & baking powder.Grease the two racks for an air-fryer oven.Put the wings onto an oiled rack or put only enough wings into a basket in a single layer.

2. Put the racks/basket into an air-fryer & cook for fifteen mins at 250 degrees F.

3. Turn the wings & switch the trays. Increase temp to 430 F. Air fry for around 15- 20 mins, till chicken wings are cooked & crispy.

18. Chicken Tikka Skewers with Creamy Avocado Sauce

Cook time: 10 mins Servings: 4 Difficulty: Hard

Ingredients

For Chicken

- 1 lb of skinless chicken thighs, boneless (slice into bite-size pieces)

- Lemon juice: 1 tbsp

- Half tsp of Sea salt

- Half tsp of Ground cumin

- Avocado mayo: 2 tbsp

- Freshly grated ginger: 1 tbsp

- 1 tsp of Chinese five-spice

- 1/4 tsp of Coriander

- 1 tsp of turmeric

- 1 and a half tsp Smoked paprika

- 2 minced cloves of garlic

Others

- Salt & pepper, to taste

- 1 bell pepper cut julienne style

- 1 onion cut into slices

- Olive oil, as needed

Avocado sauce

- Avocado oil: 2 tbsp

- Half avocado

- Cilantro leaves: 1/4 cup

- Salt, to taste

- Lime juice: 1 tbsp

- Water, as needed

- 1 clove of garlic

- Nut milk: 1/4 cup

Instructions

1. In a bowl, add chicken and all the other ingredients. Mix well and keep in the fridge for two hours.

2. Thread the chicken on skewers, add 2 to 3 pieces of chicken on every skewer.

3. Oil spray the air-fryer's basket. Put skewers in the basket in one even layer.

4. In the air-fryer basket, add onion and bell pepper slices in one layer. Pour olive oil over them and season with salt and pepper.

5. Select dual cook, and bake the first cycle for five mins at 350 degrees F.

6. Air fry the second cycle for five mins at 425 degrees F.

7. Make sure chicken is cooked, and vegetables are tender.

8. In a food processor, add all avocado sauce's ingredients and pulse till it becomes smooth.

9. As the food processor is on, add water to make it smooth; start with 2 tbsp of water.

10. Add salt to taste.

11. Serve the chicken with avocado sauce and with cauliflower rice.

Chapter No 5: Air-Fry Beef, Meat and Pork Recipes

19.　Taco Meatballs | Air-Fryer Keto Taco Meatballs

Cook Time: 15 mins Servings: 4 Difficulty: Easy

Ingredients

- Lean Ground Beef 1 lb

- Chopped onions 1/4 cup.

- Chopped Cilantro 1/4 cup.

- Minced Garlic 1 tbsp

- Taco Seasoning 2 tbsp

- Blend Shredded Cheese (Mexican) 1/2 cup

- Eggs 1

- Kosher Salt

- Ground Black Pepper

For Dipping Sauce

- sour cream 1/4 cup

- salsa 1/2 cup

- Cholula hot sauce 1-2

Instructions

1. Put all the ingredients in a mixing bowl on the stand.
   Stir till it becomes a sticky paste, around 2-3 mins,
   using a paddle attachment.

2. Form them into twelve meatballs. Put the meatballs in the basket of an Air-Fryer. For ten mins, set the Air-Fryer at 400 degrees F.

3. Meanwhile, blend the sauce: mix the salsa, hot sauce & sour cream in a bowl. Now enjoy it with the meatballs.

20. Taco Twists

Cook Time: 22 mins Servings: 4 Difficulty: Easy

Ingredients

- 1 tube of crescent rolls, refrigerated

- 1/3 pound of ground beef

- Cheddar cheese, shredded: 2/3 cup

- 1 diced onion

- Diced green chilies: 3 tbsp

- Garlic powder: 1/4 tsp

- Ground cumin: 1/8 tsp

- Salsa: 1/3 cup

- Hot pepper sauce: 1/4 tsp Salt: 1/8 tsp

Instructions

1. Let the Air-Fryer preheat to 300 degrees F.

2. In a skillet, cook onions and beef on medium flame until meat is fully cooked.

3. Add in cumin, cheese, hot pepper sauce, salsa, salt, chilies, and garlic powder.

4. Roll the dough and divide into four rectangles; put half a cup of meat in every rectangle.

5. Make four corners join with each other and twist it.

6. Place in an oil sprayed basket of Air-Fryer and cook for 18 to 22 mins, in one even layer.

7. Serve right away.

21.   Air-Fryer Asian Beef & Veggies

Cook Time: 8 min Servings; 4 Difficulty: Easy.

Ingredients

- Cut into strips sirloin steak 1 lb

- Cornstarch 2 tbsp

- Sliced yellow onion 1/2 med

- Sliced into strips red pepper one med.

- Minced garlic three cloves

- Grated ginger 2 tbsp

- Red chili flakes 1/4 tsp

- Soy sauce 1/2 cup

- Rice vinegar 1/4 cup

- Sesame oil 1 tsp

- Brown sugar 1/3 cup

- Chinese 5 spice 1 tsp

- Water 1/4 cup

Instructions

1. On a gallon-shaped zip bag, put all the ingredients. Make sure that all the ingredients are mixed. For up to four months, mark & freeze.

2. Overnight, thaw the zip bag in the freezer.

3. Remove the vegetables & steak using tongs & move them to the Air-Fryer. Take the marinade away.

4. Preheat the Air-Fryer to 400 degrees F & set the timer to 8 mins.

5. Serve with rice, then garnish with scallions & sesame seeds.

22.   **Steak Fajitas**

Cook Time: 10 mins Servings: 6 Difficulty: Easy

Ingredients

- 1 beef flank steak

- 6 tortillas, whole wheat

- 2 tomatoes, chopped without seeds

- 1 jalapeno, chopped without seeded

- Chopped red onion: half cup

- Chopped fresh cilantro: 3 tbsp

- Ground cumin: 2 tsp Lime juice: 1/4 cup

- Salt: 3/4 tsp 1 onion, cut into slices

Instructions

1. In a bowl, add jalapenos, chopped red onion, tomatoes, cilantro, lime juice with salt (1/4 tsp), cumin (1 tsp), mix well, and set it aside.

2. Let the Air-Fryer preheat to 400 degrees F.

3. Season steak with the rest of the salt and cumin.

4. Put on an oil sprayed basket of Air-Fryer and cook for 6 to 8 mins on each side until internal temperature reaches 135- 145 degrees F. keep checking for the desired doneness.

5. Take out and let it rest for five mins.

6. Air-Fryer the sliced onion for 2 to 3 mins.

7. Cut the steak into strips or shred the steak.

8. Place tortilla on a flat surface and top with salsa, onion, and steak strips.

9. Serve right away

23.   **Air-Fryer Steak Tips**

Cook Time: 20 mins Servings: 4 Difficulty: Easy

Ingredients

- Potatoes 1/2 lb

- Steaks 1 lb

- Butter 2 tbsp

- Worcestershire sauce 1 tsp

- Garlic powder 1/2 tsp

- Salt

- Black pepper

- Minced parsley for garnish

Instructions

1. Carry a pot of water to a simmer & after this, add the potatoes. Cook for five mins or till almost soft. Place away & drain

2. Combine the tips for steaks with blanched potatoes. Mix the melted butter, garlic powder, Worcestershire sauce, salt, and pepper.

3. Preheat your Air-Fryer for four mins at 400 degrees F.

4. In the Air-Fryer basket, scatter the steak & potatoes in a layer. Air fry for 10 to 18 mins at 400 degrees F, shaking & flipping & the steak & potatoes two cycles during the cooking process.

5. To see how well cooked it is, see the steak. If you want to do something about the steak, put an additional 2 to 5 mins of cooking time.

6. Sprinkle with parsley. If needed, drizzle with extra salt and pepper. Serve hot.

24.   Herb & Cheese-Stuffed Burgers

Cook Time: 16 mins Servings: 4 Difficulty: Medium

Ingredients

- 1 pound of lean ground beef

- 2 green onions, cut into thin slices

- Dijon mustard: 4 tsp

- Chopped fresh parsley: 2 tbsp

- Ketchup: 2 tbsp.

- Dried rosemary: half tsp

- 4 buns, cut in half

- Dry bread crumbs: 3 tbsp

- Dried sage leaves: 1/4 tsp

- 2 oz. of sliced cheddar cheese

- Salt: half tsp

Instructions

1. Let the Air-Fryer preheat to 375 degrees F.

2. In a bowl, mix mustard (2 tsp), green onions, and parsley.

3. In another bowl, mix mustard (2 tsp), ketchup, crumbs, and seasonings. Mix and add beef to this bowl; mix it well but do not over mix.

4. Make into eight patties. Put green onion mix and cheese slices on 4 patties.

5. Place one patty on top of the filling, seal the edges.

6. Cook in oil sprayed basket of Air-Fryer for 8 mins on one side in one even layer, carefully flip and cook for 6 to 8 mins more until internal temperature reaches 160 degrees F.

7. Place on buns and serve.

Chapter No 6: Air-Fryer Fish and Seafood Recipes

25. Fried Shrimp Po'Boy Sandwich Recipe

Cook Time: 10 mins Servings: 4 Difficulty: Easy

Ingredients

- Deveined shrimp 1 lb

- Creole seasoning 1 tsp

- Buttermilk 1/4 cup

- Louisiana fish fry coating 1/2 cup

- Cooking oil spray

- Canola or vegetable oil

- French bread hoagie rolls 4

- Shredded iceberg lettuce 2 cups

- Tomato slices 8

- Remoulade sauce

- Mayo 1/2 cup

- Minced Garlic 1 tsp

- Lemon juice 1/2

- Worcestershire 1 tsp

- Creole seasoning 1/2 tsp

- Dijon mustard 1 tsp

- Hot sauce 1 tsp

- Green onion chopped 1.

Instructions

Remoulade Sauce

1. In a small bowl, put all ingredients. Before serving, refrigerate, whereas the shrimp cook.

2. Breading and shrimp.

3. In Creole seasoning, marinate shrimp and for 30 mins buttermilk.

4. In the bowl, add fry fish. Take your shrimp from a bag & dip each into a fish fry. In the basket of air-fryer, add shrimp.

5. Spray the air-fryer basket with cooking oil. Add the shrimp to the air-fryer basket.

6. With cooking oil, spritz the shrimp.

7. Cook shrimp for 5 mins at 400 degrees F. Open the basket & flip the shrimp to the other side. Cook for another 5 mins or when crisp.

8. On the French toast, pour the remoulade sauce. After that, apply the sliced tomato and broccoli, followed by the shrimp.

26.   **Bacon Wrapped Scallops**

Cook Time: 10 mins Servings: 4 Difficulty: Easy

Ingredients

- BBQ Sauce: 1/4 cup

- 8 center-cut bacon slices

- 16 sea scallops (large)

Instructions

1. Cut bacon in half, and air fry them for 3 mins at 400 degrees F.

2. Dry the scallops well.

3. With bacon slices, wrap the scallops and seal with toothpicks.

4. Put them in the air-fryer in one even layer.

5. Brush the wrapped scallops with BBQ sauce. Or spray with oil and black pepper, and salt.

6. Air fry for five mins at 400 degrees F. flip them and brush with sauce again and cook for 5 more mins.

7. Serve right away.

27. Easy Air-fryer Fifteen Minute Crab Cakes

Cook Time: 10 mins Servings: 4 Difficulty: Easy

Ingredients

- Cooking oil

- Jumbo lump crab meat 8 ounces

- Old bay seasoning 1 tbsp

- Breadcrumbs 1/3 cup

- Cup red peppers diced.

- Green peppers diced ¼ cup

- Medium egg 1

- Mayo ¼ cup

- Lemon juice ½

- Flour 1 tsp

Instructions

1. With the cooking oil, spray an air-fryer basket.

2. Well, mix all the required ingredients except the flour.

3. Shape mixture into the four patties. To each patty, add a dash of flour.

4. Put crab cakes in Air-fryer. With cooking oil, spray crab cakes.

5. At 370 degrees F, cook for 10 mins.

6. Before serving, cool it.

28. Air-fryer Cajun Shrimp

Cook Time: 8 mins Servings: 4 Difficulty: Easy

Ingredients

- 24 peeled shrimp (extra jumbo)

- Cajun seasoning: 1 tbsp

- 1 zucchini, cut into half-moons (¼" thick)

- Olive oil: 2 tbsp

- 1 yellow squash, cut into half-moons (¼" thick)

- Kosher salt: ¼ tsp

- 6 oz of cooked chicken sausage, slices

- 1 red bell pepper, cut into 1" pieces (without seeds)

Instructions

1. In a bowl, add shrimps and Cajun seasoning, coat them well.

2. In a bowl, add vegetables, oil, and sausage and mix to combine.

3. Let the air-fryer preheat to 400 degrees F.

4. In the air-fryer basket, add shrimps and vegetable mix in one even layer.

5. Cook for 8 mins, and after 2-3 mins, shake the basket.

6. Serve right away.

29.   Air-fryer Crispy Fish Sandwich

Cook Time: 10 mins Servings: 2 Difficulty: Easy

Ingredients

- All-purpose flour 2 tbsp

- Garlic powder 1/2 tsp

- Pepper 1/4 tsp

- Salt 1/4 tsp

- Egg 1

- Fresh lemon juice 1 tbsp

- Mayo 1/2 tbsp

- Cod fillets sliced 10 oz

- Panko bread crumbs 1/2 cup

- Cooking oil

- Buns two

- Primal kitchen tartar sauce

Instructions

Breading

1. Build a cooking station. In a large bowl, put garlic powder, flour, pepper, and salt to dredge a fish.

2. Put the egg, lemon juice & mayo in to separate large bowl from dredging a fish. Whisk the egg & mix the ingredients.

3. Put the panko breadcrumbs in another bowl. Have a moist towel closely.

4. In flour, dredge a fish, then a mixture of egg & then breadcrumbs.

Air-fryer Fish

1. With the cooking oil, spray the air-fryer basket & put the fish in the basket.

2. Spritz the top area of fish with the cooking oil.

3. For crispy & golden, cook fish for eight to ten mins at four hundred degrees.

4. Whitefish is tender & delicate. Be alert if you move the fish and whereas handling it when eliminating it from the air-fryer.

30.　Tortilla Crusted Tilapia Salad

Cook Time: 15 mins Servings: 2 Difficulty: Easy

Ingredients

- Chipotle lime dressing: half cup

- 6 cups of mixed greens

- 1/3 cup of chopped red onion

- 1 cup of cherry tomatoes

- 2 Tilapia fillets (tortilla crusted)

Instructions

1. Oil spray the fish fillets on every side.

2. Put in the basket of air-fryer and cook for 15 to 18 mins at 390 degrees F. In two bowls, mix half of all vegetables, pour over the lime dressing.

3. Put fish fillet on top and serve right away.

Chapter No 7: Air-Fryer

Appetizers, Bread and Snacks

31.   Prosciutto Wrapped Brie

Cook Time: 25 mins Servings: 6 Difficulty: Easy

Ingredients

- Brie Cheese Wheel 1 Double, small

- Prosciutto 4 ounces thinly sliced

- Sugar-Free Preserves 2 tbsp

Instructions

1. In a 5" pie pan, lie prosciutto four slices.

2. Place two slices that go the other direction.

3. Over the first half, break the brie in half, sprinkle sugar-free preserves 1 tbsp, then place the latter half back on & spread the preserves on top.

4. Fill the brie with six bacon slices.

5. Bake for 20 mins at 400 degrees F, then broil 2 to 3 mins.

6. The air-fryer is set to 350 degrees F and carefully tracks. The cheese is undoubtedly melting once you see the crisping up of prosciutto. To keep the cheese in place, you would need to bring it into a tiny pan.

32.   Air-Fried Calzones

Cook time: 20 mins Servings: 2 Difficulty: Medium

Ingredients

- Baby spinach leaves: 3 cups

- Extra virgin olive oil: 1 tsp

- 6 oz. of prepared pizza dough (whole-wheat)

- Finely diced red onion: 1/4 cup

- Shredded mozzarella cheese: 6 tbsp

- Rotisserie shredded chicken breast: 1/3 cup

- Marinara sauce, low-sodium: 1/3 cup

Instructions

1. In a cast-iron skillet, heat the oil and sauté onion for 2 mins until tender.

2. Add spinach, cover the skillet and cook until it wilts for about one and a half mins. Turn off the heat, add in chicken and marinara sauce.

3. Slice the dough into four portions. Roll each piece into a six" circle.

4. Add 1/4th of the spinach mixture on the circled dough and add 1/4th of cheese on one half of the circle.

5. Fold the other half over the filling and seal the edges and crimp them.

6. Spray the calzones with oil spray.

7. Put the calzones in an oiled air-fryer basket. Cook for 12 mins at 325 degrees F until the dough is light brown. Flip the calzones and cook for 8 more mins.

8. Serve right.

33.   Air-fryer Tater Tots

Cook Time 15 mins Servings 4 Difficulty: Easy

Ingredients

- Russet potatoes 1 1/2 lbs All-purpose flour 2 tsp

- Cooking oil Salt n pepper

- Optional spices/seasoning Garlic powder 1 tsp

- Thyme 1/4 tsp Smoked paprika 1 tsp

Instructions

1. Bring a saucepan or pot 3/4 of the way full of cold water to a boil with a pinch of salt. Add enough water to cover the potatoes.

2. Add the potatoes and simmer for 6-12 mins. You should be able to pierce the potatoes easily on the outside and tell that the inside of the potatoes is still firm.

3. Remove the potatoes from the water. Dry and allow them to cool. Wait for about 10 mins.

4. Once cooled, use the large area of a cheese grater to grate the potatoes. Squeeze out any excess water from the potatoes.

5. In a bowl, place the grated potatoes with the flour & seasonings. Russet potatoes are bland. Salt according to taste. Then stir.

6. Use your hands to form tots with the mixture. I like larger tots and made 16 tater tots. You can make smaller tots if you wish.

7. Spray both sides of the tots with cooking oil. Place the tots in the air-fryer. Air fry for 10 mins at 400 degrees.

8. Open the air-fryer and flip the tots. Cook for an additional 5 mins or until the tots have reached your desired crisp.

34.   Sweet Potato Tots

Cook time: 14 mins Servings: 4 Difficulty: Hard

Ingredients

- 1 and 1/4 tsp of kosher salt, divided

- 2 small peeled sweet potatoes

- 1/8 tsp of garlic powder

- 1 tbsp of potato starch

- 3/4 cup of ketchup

Instructions

1. In a pot, add water and let it boil on high flame. Boil potatoes for 15 mins until fork tender.

2. Take them out on a plate and let them cool for 15 mins.

3. Grate the potatoes in a bowl, and mix with 1 tsp of salt, potato starch, and garlic powder.

4. Make 24 tots-like shapes from this grated potato mixture.

5. Oil Spray the air-fryer's basket. Put half of the tots in the basket in one even layer and spray them with oil spray.

6. Cook for 12-14 mins at 400 degrees F until golden brown; flip them halfway through. Take out from air-fryer and sprinkle with 1/8 tsp of salt and enjoy with ketchup.

35. **Greek Baked Feta Psiti**

Cook Time: 10 mins Servings: 4 Difficulty: Easy

Ingredients

- Feta cheese 8 ounces, in a block

- Olive oil 2 tbsp

- Crushed red pepper 1 tbsp

- Dried Oregano 1 tbsp

- Honey/Choczero Syrup for Keto 2 tbsp

Instructions

1. Cut the feta block in half and then cut half of each thinner slice to produce four pieces.

2. On a serving bowl (heatproof), arrange these.

3. Using a basting brush (silicone) to disperse the oil uniformly. With olive oil, drizzle the cheese. Then sprinkle with oregano and red pepper flakes.

4. Using a basting brush (silicone), cover with honey and uniformly scatter the honey throughout.

5. Put the dish in the basket of the air-fryer.

6. For 10 mins at 400 degrees F, set the air-fryer.

7. When finished, remove and serve with the basting brush to disperse any honey and oil that has been transferred to the bottom.

36.   Sweet Potato Chips

Cook time: 28 mins Servings: 4 Difficulty: Easy

Ingredients

- Ground Cinnamon: 1 tsp

- 2 Sweet Potatoes, cut into thin slices

- Salt & black pepper, to taste

- Extra virgin Olive Oil: ¼ cup

Instructions

1. In cold water, soak the thinly cut potatoes for half an hour.

2. Discard the water, and with paper, dry the slices. Make them completely dry so they will get crispy.

3. Coat the slices with olive oil, black pepper, cinnamon, and salt. Make sure every piece is coated with oil and seasoning.

4. Oil Spray the air-fryer's basket.

5. Air fry the slices for 20 mins at 390 degrees F, shake the basket every 7 to 8 mins.

6. Cook for an additional five mins if they are not crispy enough.

7. Serve right away with a dipping sauce.

Chapter No 8: Air-Fryer Dessert and Frittatas Recipes

37.   Air-fryer mini-Nutella doughnut holes

Cook Time: 5 mins Servings: 32 Difficulty: Easy

Ingredients

- Egg 1 large

- Water 1 tbsp

- Big refrigerated flaky biscuits one tube

- Nutella 2/3 cup

- Oil to deep-fat fry

- Sugar (confectioners)

Instructions

1. Air-fryer preheated to 300 degrees F. Beat egg with water. Roll every biscuit into the six-in. Circle on the lightly floured surface; cut every into four wedges. Brush gently with the mixture of an egg; top every wedge with one tsp of Nutella. Carry up the corners over the filling, pinch edges tightly to seal.

2. Arrange biscuits in a single layer on the tray in an air-fryer basket in the batches. Cook till its color changes to a golden brown, 8 to 10 mins, flipping once. Brush with confectioners' Sugar; serve hot.

38.   Air-fryer Donuts

Cook Time: 15 mins Servings: 8 Difficulty: Medium

Ingredients

- 1 can of large flaky biscuits

- Granulated Sugar: Half cup

- Melted unsalted butter: 4 tbsp

- Ground cinnamon: 1 tbsp

Instructions

1. In a bowl, mix cinnamon and Sugar. Set it aside.

2. Place biscuits separately on a parchment-lined baking sheet and cut one" round holes in the center.

3. Oil spray the Air-fryer's basket.

4. Put doughnuts in one even layer leaving one" inch space between, and cook for 5-6 mins at 350 degrees F, until donuts become golden brown.

5. Take donuts on a cookie sheet, and brush with melted butter, coat in the sugar-cinnamon mix.

6. Serve right away.

39.   **Air-fryer pudding**

Cook Time: 15 mins Servings: 2 Difficulty: Easy

Ingredients

- Chopped semisweet chocolate 2 ounces.

- Half-&-half cream 1/2 cup

- Sugar 2/3 cup

- Milk 1/2 cup

- Egg 1 large

- Vanilla extract 1 tsp

- Salt 1/4 tsp

- (Crusts removed & sliced into cubes) day-old bread four slices.

Instructions

1. Melt chocolate in the microwave-safe bowl, whisk till smooth. Mix in cream; set aside.

2. In the bowl, stir milk, Sugar, egg, salt & vanilla. Mix it in a mixture of chocolate. Put bread cubes & toss to cover. Let it rest for fifteen mins.

3. Air-fryer preheated to 325 degrees F. Spoon the bread combination into the two greased 8 oz ramekins. Put on a tray in an air-fryer basket. Cook till a knife inserted in the middle comes out.

4. If you like, then top it with whipped cream & confectioners' Sugar.

Chapter No 9: Air-Fry Vegetables

& Sides Recipes

40.　　Air-fryer Falafel

Cook time: 15 mins Servings: 18 Difficulty: Medium

Ingredients

Falafel

- Flour: half cup

- 1 can of drained chickpeas (15 oz.)

- White onion chopped: 1 cup

- Parsley leaves: 1 cup

- Lemon juice: 1 tbsp

- 6 cloves of garlic

- Baking powder: 1 tsp

- Cumin: 2 tsp

- Cilantro leaves: half cup

- Salt: 1 tsp

- Fresh dill leaves: ¼ cup

Instructions

1. In a food processor, add all Ingredients. Pulse on high until it forms a crumbly mixture.

2. Keep scraping the bowl, as required.

3. Take out in a bowl and keep in the fridge for one hour.

4. With a scooper, take 1 tbsp of dough and make it into falafels.

5. Oil spray the air-fryer's basket; let the air-fryer preheat to 375 degrees F.

6. Put falafels in the basket of the air-fryer in one even layer.

7. Cook at 375 degrees F for 15 mins.

8. Take out and let them cool slightly.

9. Serve with tahini sauce and hummus.

Conclusion

Air-fryer is simple to use and includes an integrated microprocessor for flawless output every time. It's designed to help your safe lifestyle. Enjoy all of your favorite deep-fried foods' rich tastes and crispy texture without the oil or mess. No more straining and dumping spent fryer oil—you will now have the same performance from as little as 2 tablespoons of oil. Don't give up the experience; give up the calories!

It's simple to use, clean, and maintain. It's also fast, flexible, and handy. Make all of your family's favorite fried foods without any of the mess or the regret. With the press of a button, you will enter a world of flavor.

It's easy-to-use touch controls. And since the Instant Air-fryer remembers the preferences, you can make your favorites at the click of a button.

The Instant Vortex Air-fryer is engineered to be quick, dependable, and safe, with the same dedication to safety and consumer loyalty.

The Air-fryer is a kitchen gadget that can blow the whole planet off its feet. The Air-fryer aims to offer a healthier alternative to the common yet unhealthy fried food. Except for fried turkey at Thanksgiving, most people do not fry at home, but the Air-fryer offers much versatility. It saves chefs by almost immediately heating food at a high temperature and rendering cooking a breeze.